# Test

## to to

# Testimony

authorHOUSE®

*Test to Testimony*

By: La-Toya Arthur-Tucker, MSc.

Edited by: Candacie Thompson

*AuthorHouse™*
*1663 Liberty Drive*
*Bloomington, IN 47403*
*www.authorhouse.com*
*Phone: 1 (800) 839-8640*

*Scripture quotations marked NIV are taken from the Holy Bible, New International Version®. NIV®. Copyright © 1973, 1978, 1984 by International Bible Society. Used by permission of Zondervan. All rights reserved. [Biblica]*

*Scripture quotations marked NKJV are taken from the New King James Version. Copyright © 1982 by Thomas Nelson, Inc. Used by permission. All rights reserved.*

*Published by AuthorHouse 07/19/2018*

*ISBN: 978-1-5462-4737-1 (sc)*
*ISBN: 978-1-5462-4736-4 (e)*

*Print information available on the last page.*

# Introduction

**\* \* \* \* \* \* \***

A well sung gospel chorus says:

*"Press along saint, press along, in God's own way,*
*persecution we must face trials and crosses in our way,*
*the hotter the battle, the sweeter the victory"*

This song is sung by many thoughtlessly until they can fully understand through experience what the words mean. Ranlene Maxim West epitomises the name of this book very aptly. It has been read, heard of, misinterpreted, enacted, and learnt. Interestingly the story of Job is still not used as an example by some when trials are present.

Hurdles began for her as a child; one would believe that her life has been destined for gloominess instead of greatness. Despite her numerous adversities, she still glitters like a true diamond. This book was compiled to encourage and remind others that regardless of the circumstances of life there will always be light at the end of the tunnel that God leads you through. Your Test can only become Testimony through Jesus Christ.

## *Always Remember.......*

*To everything there is a season, a time for every purpose under heaven. A time to be born and a time to die.*

*A time to weep and a time to laugh, A time to mourn and a time to dance.*

*A time to gain and a tome to lose, A time to gather and a time to throw away.*

## *Ecclesiastes* 3: 1, 2, 4 & 6

# *Acknowledgements*

All thanks and praises are given to God Almighty. Without Him this would not have been a reality. Special thanks are given to Ranlene who consented to disclose information about her trials and testimonies that truly made her who she is. Delroy has been very supportive. Numerous thanks to Candacie Brower-Thompson whose willing spirit is a true motivation. Junior Tucker has been a silent cheerleader and for his unlimited support, thanks are extended. His willing efforts have significantly assisted this book becoming a reality. Gratitude is extending to everyone who has made this initiative a possibility. Whether the contribution was a smile, a nod, an encouragement or a tangible support, thank you thank you and God bless!

# *Dedication*

This book is dedicated to Ranlene Maxim West. She is a stalwart mom and big sister, for this we take this opportunity to tell her how much we love her. We trust that God blesses her to experience the fruits of her hard work she invested in training us and moulding us to be who we are in society.

Additionally, special dedication is made to everyone who may be currently experiencing their trials, have experienced their trials and are thinking they are in a bubble of gloom forever. The encouragements shared should serve as reminders that your best is yet to come, keep holding on and you too will win the victory and will have a TESTIMONY!

# *Table of Content*

**✱✱✱✱✱✱✱✱**

# Chapter One

### 'The joy of two worlds'

She was the first born of both parents with six siblings from both her maternal and paternal lineages. Quite a large family, twelve siblings, two deceased; a paternal brother and a maternal sister, the other ten contribute tremendously to her tests becoming Testimonies. She has been and is still a role model to her siblings and many other individuals. Born on November 5, 1965 to Stanley Fraser and the late Lynette McLeod, Ranlene is a strong, gifted, jovial, creative, beautiful African Guyanese woman.

### *When it all started*

As the only child of her parents she innocently indulged in the pampering and love that engulfed her life. She was a mommy's girl at one time and a daddy's angel at another. She basked in the firm love they extended to her. These were great moments in her life. While her parents did not live together, the love she received proportionately filled that gap. They shared many close moments that included her and for this she was truly grateful. Like a vapour her '*only child*' title was replaced with '*older sibling*'. In her memory that title grew from faint to bold, then bolder as the siblings' number grew exponentially.

From the tender age of four she was tasked with the eldest sibling responsibilities. By age eight, her roles officially started. These motivated her to get tasks done using her initiative. She was eager to get things done as many independent eight years olds back then would have enjoyed. Her ingenuity was highly commended by her mother. This signalled the need to increase responsibilities and as such her reward was more duties and domestic chores.

### Her parental influences

Her mother worked in a 'Uniformed Force' as a cook. Her job was slightly demanding. As demanding as it was, her parental role was never hindered. Her ability to procreate was consistent with her employment attitude: filled with hard work. She was on point in extending her family. However, the more she extended the greater the responsibility was for Ranlene. While her mother was busy her father was even busier. He was multiplying just the same, leading double lives, in some instances this was done with Lynette, at other times, it was someone else.

Paradoxically, they both sought to instil the right principals and morals in Ranlene. Lynette demonstrated her parental roles in the form of a 4x100 relay; she passed the moral baton on Ranlene who then had to pass it on to her siblings. Stanley Fraser on the other hand being the trained Officer of a uniformed force found it essential to extend the same discipline to his first born daughter. She was flogged several times as a disciplinary measure. The few, though felt as many instances of physical discipline she received have etched lasting memories in her mind. These have shaped who she is to a great extent.

Ranlene's best childhood memories were experiences of Christmas. She received gifts and most desired things which were very absent throughout the year. In addition to Christmas, she received occasional birthday presents. These have stimulated her to provide for her children all that she never enjoyed. She has certainly done well for her children in ensuring that they enjoy their childhood and receive all that she was deprived.

These adult roles bestowed upon her significantly infringed negatively on her childhood enjoyment. The joy that accompanied her tasks completion was now interweaved with feelings of burden as the weight grew heavier. She had to complete her tasks by specified times her mother allotted. She performed excellently, working with the unscrupulous requests.

Her leisure time was often disrupted with shouts or calls from her mother to complete tasks she could have done herself. These requests became demands that later increased as she gained mastery in completing her assigned duties until they were solely left on her.

At eight years old, she was taking care of her younger sister and brother. She fondly recalled an unfortunate experience, having mixed her baby brother's milk too rich she gave him explosive diarrhoea. This incident prompted her mother to show her how she should mix the tea for future references. Feeding her siblings with extremely hot tea, or adding a little too much of some ingredient in their food, all evoked strong disciplinary measures.

Ranlene is now an avid cook and gives credit to her many childhood experimentations in the kitchen which have furnished her with cookery expertise as an adult. Although some provided her with physical memories of things she should refrain from. However, collectively they all contributed to her strong passion for cooking. She literally takes the kitchen over and her manoeuvre demonstrates the joy cooking erupts within her heart. The tastes express that learning has truly taken place and the accurate balance would sweep any one off their feet. She is an extremely versatile cook, with no recipe off limits and when she is finished, no one can tell that a cook was present, except for the appetizing aroma. Ranlene's kitchen is always immaculate during her food preparations, a practice she still upholds to this day.

### Terrible Childhood Accident

Ranlene sought every opportunity to engage in childhood activities. This often resulted in her being reprimanded or physically punished. To her the benefits outweighed the cost and she was willing to trade punishment after brief moments of childhood joy. Unfortunately, her mother was obviously oblivious that innocent fun and happy moments was all she yearned for. One evening while her mother was busy engaged in preparations for a wedding, Ranlene seized the opportunity to played ring games with her friends. It was going well until the screams of a parent was heard. It was a father's call. "Alicia[1]! Alicia!" While Ranlene's heart was filled with fear there was a slight relief hearing a different name. It was now revealed that Ranlene was not the only one having childhood fun sneakily. The parent called angrily for his daughter who was too captivated in fun to answer her daddy's call. He saw her in the ring and decided to punish her greatly. He strapped a hammer and a chisel together and he aimed the two tools to throw at her. The children were running around in a circle. As he threw the two tools, his daughter ran passed not knowing what was being thrown or even

---

[1] This is a fictitious name

happening and Ranlene was next in line, Bang! She was knocked down, she fell like a tree chopped by an axe. She was totally unconscious. She regained consciousness vomiting blood. The father's rage was laced with fear as he realised it was not his daughter he hit. Many wonder if the reaction he expressed would have been the same if Alicia was hit. Ranlene's mother was called, she wept uncontrollably after seeing the state of her daughter. The matter was subsequently resolved amicably after Alicia's father begged profusely. What do you think happened next? As you may have guessed, his apologies were accepted and to avoid publicity, Ranlene was regrettably not even taken to the hospital. Lynette was a peacemaker, but the gravity of this situation warranted firm and appropriate action. Ranlene receive some home treatment and before long, her domestic responsibilities had resumed.

# "Anger brings Accidental blow"

## Test

This accident could have been fatal. It could have been Ranlene's head that was hit. So many things could have happened. The tools hit Ranlene at her side.

## Testimony

God while allowing the incident to happen, protected Ranlene, he knew there was a long journey ahead of her, as this book would reveal, He healed her and granted a speedy recovery. No rib or any body part was broken. Thanks and ALL praises be to God!

**Jeremiah 29:11** – *For I know the thoughts that I think toward you, says the Lord, thoughts of peace and nit of evil, to give you a future and a hope.*

## Academic Decline

As Ranlene grew older, her school attendance became less frequent. She was absent many days trying to get things sorted for her siblings. They had to be prepared for school, be given snacks, after which she had to get herself ready. Obviously, by the time she was through with them, she was late for her school. Her chronic late attendances attracted punishment by her teachers. Ranlene was not pleased at this. Punishments at home and punishment at school were certainly not adding up. Like the average child her age did, she tried to evade the punishments and started staying away from school. This made her a truant. Since her attendance and punctuality were very inconsistent, her learning aligned itself with the two inconsistencies. She now had a dislike for learning. She attended school, marked her name then left school. This went on for weeks until a friend of her mother saw her. Her activities came to an abrupt end with a fine whipping by her mother. In those days parents were not afraid to complain to other parents about their children. Therefore, the moment Ranlene saw Ms B she knew her fun had just ended. Thanks to Ms B going to lucky pool[2] was no longer part of her enjoyment.

Her academic performance continued on a downward spiral and no one noticed. Then one day, an observant school teacher realising something was amidst started focussing on her. She acted out several times at school. While she was an expressive child, her expressions were more pronounced. There were instances where she worked hard and wished she did better and there were other times where her performance meant nothing to her.

**Fraudulent Abilities Recognised**

With her consistently poor grades Ranlene's academic performance was no longer a surprise to her mother. However, amidst her consistently poor grades, she had the intrinsic motivation to improve. One school term, Ranlene took a black ink pen and sought to reverse her poor performance on her report card to an above average one. There was fourteen percent in English; she turned the one into a nine thus giving her ninety four out

---

[2] This can be found at this location

of a hundred. She did this reversal with other subjects where the numbers were flexible. Her mother having glimpsed through the grades were surprised at the sudden improvement and commended her for her high performance. Mr. Felix, a good friend of her mother visited the family and requested her report card as he did on a termly basis. Upon inspection of it he realised, the ingenious acts of Ranlene. This became obvious to him since the comments the class teacher made were not a reflection of the grades. There was a clear disconnect between the grades shown and the class average, Teachers' comments and overall performance. This was immediately brought to her mother's attention and as usual she was punished. All the punishments Ranlene received made her glide down the path of misbehaviour more easily. She misbehaved to get attention and her true aim was trivialised.

Her non-performance became evident as she scored marks to attend Lodge Government School now Lodge Secondary School. This was the commencement of another era for her. She started realising her potentials and aimed to improve at the Secondary School Entrance

Examination (SSEE) exams. This was not realised and her grade was never known since no one went to uplift her results. This was the official school leaving process for Ranlene.

## *Party Organiser*

Childhood parties were only imaginations. As Ranlene grew older she had it all planned out and ready to make it a reality. She wanted a party so badly that she began organising one. This was done without the inclusion of her parents. She was still but a child when she made these plans. Reality check revealed that she had no money to purchase the things for the party. However, Ranlene had a backup plan. She went into her mother's purse and saw six dollars and five cents ($6.05c). From her estimation the five dollars would have covered her expenses better so that's what she stole. Lynette later realised her money was stolen so she was planning a physical punishment for Ranlene while the party was being planned. When she was ready to go shopping, she was interrupted and her friends went without her.

She was corporally punished and all her plans, organising and labour went to the benefit of her friends.

They heard her screams and really could not help her. Ranlene received the discipline for this act from her father. Perhaps if she had spoken and confessed to stealing the money the flogging might not have been so severe but she held out and refused to admit, until after she received the first lash. The other lashes followed mainly because her parents instilled, 'honesty is the best policy' within their teachings. Her party had ice-cream, bubble gums, sweets, biscuits and different sodas. They all had a blast except the event organiser.

### Saved by the smell

Lynette was super tired. As many parents are, they ask their child or children to sleep while they sleep. This is done often when the child or children are very young. So Ranlene was asked to sleep. Did she sleep? Well, well, she decided to light a garbage heap beneath their house. They lived in an apartment building with a small space underneath; the average child had to bend to enter under the building. Ranlene took papers and decided to light them afire. "No man, dis ting tekkin too long to finish bun" she thought. "Maybe I should add sum cloth dat cud speed up de blaze" This was exactly what she did. She went to a neighbouring tailor shop collected the scraps and she added same. This fuelled the fire nicely that eventually went out of control. She dashed to the pipe and return to the blaze with mouthfuls of water that were very useless. She quickly sneaked back in the room and pretended to be asleep.

The smoke started to move through the apartment rooms, neighbours raised the alarm and the fire was quickly extinguished. No one knew who the culprit was. Ranlene pretended for a little while longer after which she faked a stretch and indicated that she was up.

# "Saved by the Smoke"

# Test

A fire was started by Ranlene's childhood mischievous actions. The fire could have destroyed the entire building that could have landed several families approximately over fifty persons were housed there, homeless.

# Testimony

Thank God! An alert resident was able to sound the alarm and solicit the assistance of other residents who quickly extinguished the blaze. A childhood mischief has proven that even in our mischief God sees beyond our limitations.

**Ephesians 2:4 , 5** – *But God who is rich in mercy, because of His great love with which He loved us even when we were dead in trespasses, made us alive together with Christ (by grace you have been saved.)*

Parent Teachers' Meetings were a regular feature on her agenda. Though she was a child, she attended the meetings representing her siblings well. While she represented them, her personal representation kept either dormant or very poor.

Every day at school was now described as a hard one. It was hard; all the content taught just could not permeate Ranlene's brain. She often reached her saturation point very quickly and this would frustrate her immensely. One day while on her way home from another hard day at school, she was greeted by a panting neighbour. Neighbour explained that her brother Garfield was involved in an accident while at home and his guts were coming out. Apparently she was a bit too dramatic and expressive. Garfield was sliding down the wooded rails that held up the stairs, commonly known as a 'banister' and he slid through the stairs landing on a bean that resulted in him bursting his chin. Lynette was too emotionally weak to take him to the hospital and big sister, mother, now nurse; Ranlene had to take him to the hospital and care for him even more.

As Garfield recuperated the memory of how his big sister helped him quickly faded; his disobedient, rebellious and rude behaviour took dominance over being grateful. His teenage years brought several challenges that further perplexed Ranlene's call to duty. One day she was home caring for the other siblings when she heard a running in the yard that later came up the stairs. As she went to see who it was, it was one of his friends. The young man almost on the verge of tears explained; "police juss juss gawn wid Garvy". Troubled, Ranlene immediately went to the nearest Police station where she thought he would have been taken. As she enquired she was told that no one with that description was taken there. She started getting nervous and was subsequently advised to wait. As she was about to go, she saw the patrol vehicle but she did not see her brother. After everyone came out she heard her brother's voice. He was at the bottom of the vehicle and the other boys were asked to lie on top of him.

Garfield loved gambling, which was harshly punished in those days. He claimed he was not gambling at the time of the police patrol but was present; the police collected the gamblers and warned the onlookers. However, one gambler's shoe was left out of the vehicle. Garfield in an effort to help threw it in the police vehicle. The Police not knowing it was someone from in the vehicle shoe, thought Garfield threw a shoe at them in disrespect. He then threw the shoe out, Garfield without explaining anything threw it back in. This went on a few times and the Police Officer in an effort to utilise his power demanded him to go in the vehicle. To punish him, he placed all the gamblers on top of him and the officers drove around with them then took them to the station.

While many persons knew Ranlene was not the parent she became well known through her siblings. This was now cemented as part of her duties. In some instances the individuals came to her instead of their mother. There was another instance while Ranlene was cooking and the Head teacher sent to call Garfield's big sister. Ranlene told the messenger that their mother was home, "Ran---lin come nah you go..... ah can't manage dese sudden news," Lynette responded. Ranlene had to discontinue cooking to go, Garfield was kneeling at the school's office with his hands in the air. The Head teacher mentioned, "Garfield was brought to the school by two police officers, he was caught shoplifting". Garfield shoplifted a biscuit when asked why he did it, he responded, "cause I de hungry". Garfield had to go home for his lunch as he did daily but this day in question he decided to do otherwise. Ranlene dealt with the situation and returned home. Lynette eagerly awaited a report then mentioned, "God bless di day ah mek yuh, wuh ah gun do widout yuh meh chile". Ranlene completed her meal, everyone ate and was satisfied.

Garfield continued giving his big sister thrills, from getting away to go swimming to fighting, he had her on her heels. Oh, he certainly was not the only one who did this, while she was on her heels with him, her sisters had her on her toes. Malinie, the fifth sibling was equally mischievous for her age. She often returned home with some part of her school uniform missing. She was very saucy and still is. Her fashion skills took form until she reached adolescence. Throughout the elementary stages of her life she was totally careless about her physical appearance. She was properly dressed and sent to school, but things took a turn as she entered the school compound. One day she went home with a letter from the school. Ranlene was excited to have received a letter of commendation about her sister. As she opened, she realised her sister was selected as a "needy student" as such, the class teacher recommended her for public assistance. This was unbelievable since Laundiss her older sister attending the same school was classified differently. Malinie was always expressive, dramatic and she definitely knew how to capture and maintain the crowd's attention.

One day it was just around noon when Malinie came home crying wearing only one shoe. Ranlene furiously asked what was wrong. She explained that she rested her head on the table for a brief moment that lasted about an hour then she realised her shoe was off. Ranlene returned to the school with Malinie and Laundiss. The other students related to Ranlene that Malinie slept all morning at school and another student took off her shoe and threw it in the burial ground. St. Sidwell's Primary situated on Vlissengen and Hadfield streets Georgetown, Guyana is just beside a burial ground. Ranlene went to the school found the boy and had a quick little talk with him. He and Malinie both wore 'batta'[3]. Coincidentally they wore the same size as well. Ranlene took off the matching side of the boy's shoe and replaced Malinie's pair. The little boy was then sent in the burial ground for Malinie's one side to complete his pair.

All of these happened to Ranlene while she was still but a teenager. Despite these tests she never sought to run away or harm any of her siblings. She instead faced her tests and victoriously turned them into sweet testimonies. Nothing was too big for her to manage. She was not afraid of anyone irrespective of their ages. She experienced in some instances the joy of two worlds: Childhood and Adulthood. Her responsibilities prepared her well for the many hurdles of life; great and small she has conquered them all only through Jesus Christ.

---

[3] This was a type of shoe made of cloth associated with the lower economic class.

# *Chapter Two*

## "Doing it on my own"

The sweetness of life started and was now being unveiled for Ranlene as she reached young adulthood. Not only was she a biological parent but she also started managing herself and the domestic duties better. This felt really lovely and life was now heading down the comfort zone. She experienced life as a normal female for once. Imagine the excitement she felt, being able to go to parties and social activities like the average female.

In an interesting twist of events, her second sister was asked to leave their home by their mother. This meant there were fewer conflicts at home. Michelle often used Ranlene's personal items as many sisters did and still do and this aggravated Ranlene. Whenever she objected, it resulted in heated arguments that sometimes ended in fights. Michelle was rebellious, disrespectful and rude. Her behaviour propelled her mother to ask her to leave. She left reluctantly since she had nowhere to go. Instead of her getting better, her freedom propelled her further down the negative path of errant and complacent behaviour. She became pregnant and subsequently discharged herself after delivery leaving the innocent baby girl in the hospital. The baby's paternal grandparent and relatives cared for her from then to adolescence. She became pregnant a second time, for another man, of course, this time with her son. His paternal grandparents did the same thing as her daughter's grandparents. So Michelle's two children were raised in different geographic regions by their father's relatives, separated by time and space. The girl was raised in Georgetown, region four (4) and the boy was raised in Linden, Region ten (10). The distance between the two regions is approximately one hour and thirty by car or bus.

Before now, whenever Ranlene sought permission to go anywhere, her mother requested her taking her siblings. Her friends refused to go out with her since going with her meant the company of five little children as well. Neither Ranlene nor her friends had any children so they were not pleased with the unwanted company. This forced Ranlene to stay at home most of the time. She was a baptized Christian but this was only according to the records on the baptismal certificate. She did not fully understand her responsibilities as a Christian and even if she did, she was determined to 'enjoy life'.

### *Irregular but enjoyable social activities*

Easter Monday[4] was well anticipated by her siblings. On this day, Ranlene treated them to picnic and kite flying activities. She cooked, prepared baskets and they all had enjoyable times. Sometimes her friends went with her since these were usually public family times. Ranlene would sometimes take her cousins as well. The children within her family circle looked forward to these outings. They sometimes went to 'Chinese New Year'[5] While going out was infrequent; the few instances they went were very well received.

---

[4] Many Christians around the world celebrate Easter Monday as a day of rest, particularly in countries where the day is a public holiday. Guyana celebrates Easter Monday as a National Holiday.
[5] A time of the day where Chinese within Guyana would usher in their new year, they danced and engaged in celebratory activities.

*Ranlene semi-formally dressed at a party. She was only 19 years old.*

*A New Era of her Life*

Ranlene attended a cousin's wedding and was escorted by a stout young man. He was slightly brown in complexion seemed very reserved. He was and still is a man of few words. Ranlene as everyone knows was the spice to their interaction. Their conversations increased and so did their connection. They started dating and the relationship intensified. Although he had some bad habits, she encouraged him to make adjustments. He was a chain smoker[6] and he still is same. Ranlene wished he had stopped. He made several promises and plans but were they what she desired? Only time will tell.

Was she truly prepared to be a mother? Well, truth be told whether or not she was, the reality existed; an innocent life was growing inside her womb. The smooth sailing experienced earlier in the relationship began to encounter hurdles intermittently. As the relationship waves came, 'this too shall pass,' she thought but it really passed and sent bigger waves. Promiscuity, verbal abuse, disrespect, dishonesty, little or no financial support were just a few of the struggles she

---

[6] Someone who smokes cigarettes one after another, (Cambridge Dictionary

experienced with her partner who was the father of her unborn child. These challenges grew from simple to complex quite rapidly and Ranlene was definitely not prepared to manage them. Her options were limited mainly because of her inexperience, poor social support, and high stress level from her family of origin, physical development, and mental state of mind. These limitations propelled her to engage in countless verbal fights and arguments. There were a few instances where she included her prospective child's father in some civil discussions. These were all greeted with unpleasant attitudes and much scoff. She had reached her threshold and decided before the child was born that the relationship was over, she endured enough! Even though she informed the young man of her decision to end the relationship, his attitudes and unacceptable behaviour remained the same. He took her for granted as he usually did and he also had enough females to quickly replace her.

Ranlene endured long nights and very uncomfortable days. She was still tasked with caring for her siblings despite her pregnancy. Her pregnancy was an awakening moment; she saw things from many different perspectives. Her mother was disappointed mainly because the care of her children would be infringed. She was not upset at the choice because of Ranlene's age, but rather because it threatened Ranlene's responsibility as a Caregiver. Her mom thought she could have continued a bit longer before starting her own family.

One afternoon the frustrations were really overwhelming for Ranlene and she sat in despondency as she thought a way out. She made her way to an office in secrecy. She went to seek the assistance of a professional. She did not convey this to anyone to avoid them trying to dissuade her attempts. When she reached the office, the Secretary informed her that the individual was out of the country and she would not be able to get an appointment. She was only able to confirm an appointment for the next three days. The doctor Ranlene wanted to see was a well-known Gynaecologist. Ooops did she really want to do that? Well Yes! She wanted to do an **ABORTION**. Frustration can be exacerbated by limited or no support system, often resulting in poor decisions.  She felt a sense of guilt after she reflected on what she did.  She purposed never to make such poor decisions in her life again. She did not share this with her daughter until twenty-nine years after.   La-Toya was not upset or embarrassed at her mother for sharing.  She was pleased that her mother was courageous and open to share a secret which haunted her for years; and she was very happy that her mother was proud of her. Ranlene shared the memory to a group of individuals who were contemplating abortion as an option, her testimony has influenced the young ladies to rethink their decisions and trust God and only Him for solutions.

## *"From Frustration to Abortion"*

## *Test*

Ranlene was terribly overwhelmed with all the struggles she had in her life. At this particular time of her life while she did not think the conception of her child had contributed heavily to her stress, her child's father attitude and behaviour had influenced this poor choice. Her situation influenced her choice for an abortion.

## *Testimony*

Abortion was never an option God had planned for Ranlene. She allowed the influences of the enemy to lead her to the Doctor. God allowed the Doctor to be unavailable. He had plans for Ranlene and that unborn child. In her innocent yet frustrating state God provided a way out. God is simply awesome!

**Jeremiah 139:13  For** *You formed my inward parts;*
*You covered me in my mother's womb.*

The Doctor's absence allowed her child father to understand how much she was hurting and he started supporting a little more. Ranlene's decision was still final; she took the disappointment as an opportunity to embrace her challenges. By this she was now prepared to be the best mother she can be to her daughter. She was more grateful than ever for life and she expectantly waited for the time where she would see her first child.

The morning started with lots of work for Ranlene. She felt quite energetic and as the entire house was cleaned, 'kittle trim'[7] as some folks would say. After cleaning she was a bit tired, but then she remembered she promised her aunt Faye to spend a night with her so she kept her promise. As she arrived at her aunt's home, she described her feeling as unusual. Understanding that she was pregnant she was closely monitored. The feelings persisted as pains intensified. She was then taken to the hospital where she was admitted and early the Sunday morning on March 17, a few hours later, a beautiful baby girl was born. Ranlene named her La-Toya. She held her

---

[7] A Guyanese term that means extremely clean.

closely and had absolutely no regrets of bringing her first born into the world. Godfrey Arthur was proud to have his first daughter. He stayed a little bit longer around Ranlene and for the first time he had given her a substantial amount of money.

The money, attention and time he shared were meaningful and well appreciated, but not enough for her to change her mind. She was still adamant that the relationship was over. Her decision became evident to him when he realised that she was making strides without him. She moved on with her life. She was now officially a single mother. Life for Ranlene had taken a different turn. While her siblings had their mother around, she was now the mother, who was solely responsible for her own. Her previous trials have prepared and shaped her to a great extent. She sought a better job and she was on the road to being a responsible mother. There was a new feeling of optimism. She restarted attending parties, her daughter was growing healthily and she was getting emotionally strong.

Her friends invited her to a party and she happily accepted the invitation. She was working now so she was able to dress and feel confident. One day while attending a party, something happened that changed her life forever. She met a tall, dark handsome gentleman. From the moment she saw him, her heart melted. Something was different about him. For the entire first half of the party they kept sharing stares with each other. Smiles and other body gestures were exchanged and understood. Before long, her friends observed what was happening and they encouraged an introduction. It became evident that this couple was just waiting on the prompt. For the entire second half of the party they conversed with each other.

Just about two hours revealed that Ranlene and David had so much in common. They were both recently out of relationships with their partners being the parent of their children. They both had daughters who were born the same year. The daughters were the first born for both individuals. The connection felt so genuine and intertwined, it seemed like a happily ever after tale. They agreed to take things slowly. During the following months they grew closer as they got to know each other better. David was a serious man who knew exactly what he wanted, without any preamble and ruffle he proposed, "Ranlene, will you marry me?" while it was not this formal, she boldly responded in her informal term, "Yes I will" Well...... the rest is history and they were set to be married. Godfrey heard about the proposal and he came with one that was dramatic, promising and quite convincing but Ranlene had already said *'I will'* to another man.

On December 28, 1987, Ranlene Fraser became Ranlene West. David loved and cherished his bride. He was determined to provide her with happiness and he went the very extra mile. Lynette and Ranlene started engaging in frequent disagreements. In addition to her being married, the conflicts influenced the West Family to move to a new place of residency. After a brief stay in Durban Street Wortmanville where they stayed with David's sister and her family, they then moved to Wakenaam Essequibo[8]. Moving to Essequibo meant that they lived with the Wests family. This new experience introduced several culture shocks to Ranlene. She

---

[8] Region 7.

embraced them all, since she was prepared to make her marriage work. One day her siblings came to enjoy holidays with her family and they shared some very disheartening stories with her. She was caught between a rock and a hard place. She mustered enough strength to visit her home of origin. When she saw her mother she was moved emotionally. Her mother was not well. This caused her to return to Georgetown and she cared for her mother and her siblings.

Time progressed nicely. Wedding anniversaries went by and no addition was made to the West family. This did not bother Ranlene since her quiver was already filled with her siblings and child. Things took a turn for the negative as her mother's health deteriorated.

Lynette realised that she was not getting better and the possibility was more on the side of her dying. "Ranlin meh chile, it is not my will to die, but yuh modda nah gun mek it, God knows best." This tore Ranlene apart inside out. She could not take it, she was inconsolable. Lynette requested to be taken to Belladrum

Berbice[9] for her eldest Sister Emelda to care for her. She was taken there the Wednesday and by midday on Friday, a cousin delivered the death news……. It rung like an echo in Ranlene's ears, "Sis Lynette, your mother died this morning" What, why now, why her, who said so……… the questions came and there was no one to answer Ranlene. Was this a dream or my imagination? She just could not understand this. She enjoyed happy moments just December 1987 and her mother died 1989. God! Are you for real? She thought enjoyment of life was only for a chosen few that certainly did not include her.

---

[9] Region 5 – Mahaica-Berbice, Guyana.

# *Chapter Three*

## "The broken family circle"

**H**aving lost her mother, life changed drastically. Lynette's death took Ranlene by surprise. As absent as she was from the life of her children, Ranlene had grown accustom to her inactivity while maintaining physical presence. She plunged into severe grief. Adding to this grief was the total responsibility for her siblings. Ranlene's aunts willingly requested taking her siblings but they were going to be separated from each other. Without even thinking she boldly objected to that recommendation. She saw too many families suffer because of that decision to separate them. This motivated her to respond with great confidence as she told her aunts; "Even if we have to eat salt and rice we will survive as a whole". Her youngest sister being only seven months, her daughter 4, brothers 6 and 16, sisters,

12, 14 and 21. She was just 24. This seemed virtually impossible but Ranlene saw possibilities. She purposed to take excellent care of her siblings and she received total support from her loving husband.

Clothing and feeding her brothers and sisters were not totally her responsibility especially for the four younger ones. She was assisted by her father with two of her sisters and the father of the last two contributed as well. However, the burden of training, discipline and guidance entirely remained with her. As young as she was, she did all she knew was correct. There were many hurdles and rough sections of this new journey but she never gave up. She heavily relied on God, though she was not a committed Christian.

There were days when life seemed extremely hard for her. Her last sister was very sick. Ranlene had several troubling days with her. Many individuals pronounced death sentences on her. Others gave her time frame to remain alive, amidst everything, she never lost hope and her supportive husband stood strongly beside her. One young lady referred to her as 'it's alive'. Stacey commonly called Micey never received breast milk.

When her mother died she was innocent and still being in her infancy stage provided her with absolutely no recollection of her mother. The only mother's love she knew was that received from Ranlene. A grown woman named Daphne Edwards, also known as Sis. Eddy advised Ranlene to dedicate Stacey to God. "Girl from the time you give that baby to God, all your headaches will be over". Acknowledging her desperation and inexperience she readily followed the suggestion. This was really another testimony from the time Stacey was dedicated, her sickness started to decrease as she grew older.

There were days when Stacey would swell, she had a constant cold and her tiny body went through severe pains. While her siblings wanted to help, all they could have done was pray and hope for the best. Her tiny body at times seemed as it was ready to give up. She received lots of love, affection, attention from everyone within her immediate environment. There was never a time where she was mistreated or unattended by her older siblings around. She was loved by them all and they did their best to ensure that Micey was happy. She was the only immediate memory of their mother. This encouraged closeness among the siblings and her. They already experienced a lot, losing their baby sister was not one of their options.

Things took a different turn after the death of the mother. Ranlene led her family spiritually. She accepted the call and was baptized and two of her sisters accepted Jesus and happily followed the example she provided. This was a new path but they were determined to hold strongly unto Jesus since they were comforted by what the Bible taught. They all decided there was no better option than to serve God and to do it wholeheartedly.

When the family started attending church they were very much unable to maintain church clothing. They hadn't any to start with. From the baby to the eldest sibling, the only family who had church clothes was La-Toya. From her toddler years she was sent to church with a neighbour so she was exposed to church going. The Seventh-day Adventist church is a blessed organisation. It is usually equipped with members of all trades, and Olivet was no different. A seamstress recognising the need stepped up to the challenge and contributed lovely church dresses for Stacey. Sis Jackson ensured that the baby was always looking beautiful. Other church members worked as a team and clothes were provided for the family. Each family member was now able to change their clothes on a weekly and not quarterly basis.

Ranlene encouraged and reminded her sisters weekly that they were serving God and not man. One Sabbath morning while on their way to church, a community member having observed Malinie on her way to school and church separately for several weeks stopped her to ask a question, "Why do you wear your school shoes to church?" This humiliated Malinie and she wanted to be rude but Ranlene intervened and dealt with the situation quite nicely. As upset as Ranlene was she did not allow her emotions to conquer her desire to represent Christ in all that she did. The curious teenager became an acquaintance to the family eventually.

Her siblings were taunted many times at school but this did not influence them getting into illicit practices to earn money. They understood the family struggles and they were grateful for what they had.

Aside from 'hand me downs' they did not have any other trending styles. They either wore the clothing long after it was in style or before the style was modified and in fashion. Ranlene was chief old fashionista, she wore styles that did not even exist, she mixed and matched and ensured that she was decently attired. They were times she even wore gents clothing not because she wanted to but because she did not know and even if she knew she hadn't any other.

# "Surprise pregnancy and a healthy baby"

## Test

Stacey was extremely sick and terribly small, hence her call name Micey. Her mother was sick with her and did not know that she was pregnant. At seven months pregnant, doctors were confused at her body rejecting medication or manifesting unusual signs than those in alignment with her complaint. Tests revealed she was pregnant, not only pregnant but seven months.

## Testimony

Stacey was healthily delivered. Her mother was advised not to breast feed her because of her illness. Stacey was cared for and was a healthy baby born on February 23, 1989. She is now married and has a son.

**Job 19:25.** *"For I know that my Redeemer lives and He shall stand at last on the earth"*

David and Ranlene strategized how they would collaboratively earn to make ends meet. The struggle was real. There were conflicts, disagreements and varied challenges but they stuck together as a team and through thick and thin achieved their goals. There was never a day when anyone was hungry, unable to go to school or any need was not provided for. Thanks be to God Almighty.

Ranlene started enjoying life a little better. There was the need to celebrate, not only have they enjoyed five years of marriage going six shortly but she was pregnant. David grew even happier when he received the news. This made him show greater appreciation for his wife. He was already a romantic man and this increased his romantic expressions.

Growing plants was something his wife enjoyed. She had different plant species that she cared for in addition to her numerous responsibilities. One afternoon she was upstairs and she heard a noise downstairs. Upon checking she realised some goats were feasting on a well-cared for plant. She instinctively reached for an object and ran a short distance to pelt the goat. There was a bang! The goats ran franticly out of the yard, after the sound was heard. The bang that was heard came after Ranlene slipped and landed on her tummy. She immediately started bleeding. Oh no! This was really painful psychologically. She had a miscarriage! Without any professional therapeutic help, Ranlene took about three months to overcome the grief experienced with that loss. La-Toya was disappointed that she did not receive a sibling but flaunted the only child title a little longer.

Ranlene spent many time on her knees. She talked with God consistently. She was motivated and from some uplifting talks she was ready and rearing to go reproduce again. One of the thoughts that fuelled her joy was weeping may endure but for a night but joy comes in the morning. She was also told that other babies come quickly after a miscarriage. She said goodbye to 1991 with great hope for the upcoming years ahead.

She began the following year excitedly. They did not have to wait a very long time at all. The year nineteen hundred and ninety-two (1992) was a very prosperous one for her family. She conceived and delivered within the same year. Delroy David West was born on

December 5, 1992. Her first and only son was delivered on the Sabbath morning bright and early. The entire family was elated and were all happy to see Delroy. La-Toya was super excited to meet her brother. She had so many plans for this baby.

Delroy was now Prince charming. He was awaken from his sleep by kisses and he went to sleep with same. Not even a fly was able to light on him. He was the centre of the family's attention. Ranlene encountered a challenge during delivery and Delroy's head was squeezed. The elongated look of his head for the first two weeks did not interfere with the love the family lavished on him. La-Toya was surprised to see his head but she loved her brother very much.

## *"Only God knows everything best"*

# Test

Ranlene experience that unfortunate accident after she miss-averaged in her attempt to stone a goat. Whether or not this was a punishment for her being unkind to the animal, it was a very trying experience for her. This was a great loss. She expectantly awaited this pregnancy and it was taken from her, all because of a silly goat.

# Testimony

While she was still gliding in the gloom of the miscarriage, she discovered that she was again pregnant. This was indeed a reason to celebrate and it has truly been a testimony.

**1 Corinthians 10:13** *"No temptation has overtaken you except such as is common to man; but God is faithful, who will not allow you to be tempted beyond what you are able but with the temptation will also make the way of escape that you may be able to bear it."*

Everyone had something in stored for Delroy. His father had the biggest and best plans for him as his first matrimonial child and first man child. Mr. West did not even want Delroy to sleep. He grinned uncontrollably when persons told him Delroy looked exactly like him, and he really did.

Ranlene and David West acquired their land and they commenced building construction. He was determined that his son and the entire family should have a better life than the one they currently enjoyed. The family lived in a one bedroom house; they were pretty comfortable despite their limitations. Many Sundays the family utilised going to the land as a picnic experience. They packed their bags and food and started work very early on the land. The little children did the light work while the older ones were very much involved in the duties that attracted payments. Everyone looked forward to Sundays for the involvement in the family activities.

The afternoon was cool and they felt very happy. Eventually, the foundation was completed. Thanks be to God! As the foundation was completed, David West started experiencing chest discomfort. His wife later realised, it was an asthma attack that he had experienced. His pumps were not in his possession and he had severe asthma. He insisted that he will be fine if he just reached home and was able to relax. He was rushed home and Ranlene hadn't a clue that this was the beginning of a new chapter of her life. What will it unfold? It was only God who knew the answer.

# Chapter Four

## "When it Rains it pours"

**R**anlene now had a sick husband to care for added to her list of individuals she had to care for previously. David received his asthma medication but his condition worsened with another diagnosis. From foot pain to chest pain, joint pain it was now diagnosed that he had prostate cancer, this was experienced by his inability to urinate. His sickness debilitated Ranlene.

She greeted every day with a sigh of disgust. How much longer Lord? She often questioned. She was awakened by her sweetheart one morning; the stillness of day was all she could feel. The stillness was disturbed with a touch, then there was a soft whisper, "Honey, yuh wake up yet?' David asked, "Something is wrong, ah juss can't feel anyting on dis wan side." As Ranlene turned on the light and examine her husband, she realised his entire left side was paralyzed. Arrangements were made for him to be taken to the hospital where he was diagnosis with his first attack of stroke. This was the onset of a myriad of troubles. This was his most recent addition to the sickness collage: an attack of stroke on his left side.

During his sickness Ranlene was forced to seek employment to care for the family. This was extremely difficult for her. She had to work long hours to ensure that ends meet at home. Many days she was exhausted but no one knew. She kept her feelings secret. This affected her greatly! She kept a strong image for her children and siblings. Amidst all the struggles Delroy was only a baby. Despite everything he was healthy and active. Everyone had their needs met and things were under control. Praises be to God!

His sickness has raised unnecessary attention from his mother and her relatives. They had an antagonistic relationship ever since he started dating Ranlene since his mother disliked his preference. He expressed his desire to proceed with his life with his chosen female – Ranlene, his mother was further displeased. She used this opportunity with his sickness to belch her displeasure and concerns. The antagonism was then transferred from her son to his wife. The struggle was really on for Ranlene. Mary Jane, the mother of David West started blaming Ranlene for what was happening. She told everyone that her son was overworking to care for his wife and her siblings. This bothered Ranlene tremendously. While this was not the case, understanding the amount of stress her body and mind was under, she started thinking how things could have been differently done.

Test and trials really come in different shape and form. Ranlene lost a significant amount of weight. She was at her wits end. Life seemed painful for her. One person said if you think life is hard try death. She has never thought of suicide, thank God! Her thoughts were between her and God. She refused to engage in conversation with anyone. She prayed and prayed consistently, many times she asked God why, Why me Lord?

As Charlie's sickness further deteriorated, Mary Jane[10] decided she wanted to intervene. In his healthy state he would not have approved her decision but she capitalised on his physical inabilities. She took him to an "obeah man[11]" whom she referred to as her spiritual doctor. The persons performed several rituals on him and he was returned to his matrimonial home with great objection to Ranlene and the rest of the family praying and serving God.

This tug of war lasted a short while with Mary Jane and Ranlene while Mr. West remained in the middle. He demanded going to see his wife one Saturday and as such he was brought to the Olivet Seventh-day Adventist church. From the time he came through the door, he exhibited a very rebellious attitude. He started saying things that were very inaccurate. The church immediately paused and started a season of prayer for David West and his family. The family was surrounded by church members while Charlie was at the center. The prayers came continuously from members, as the prayers

---

[10] Name change
[11] An adept or leader in the practice of obeah: witch doctor

ascended it was the more he rebelled and started saying rude things, He was asked to repeat the words of Psalm 23 and he said " The Lord is not my shepherd and I shall always be in want" those words among other things were shared. One church sister dealt him several boxes on his face and demanded that he be freed in Jesus name. He started hallucinating and cried uncontrollably; calling persons who were not there and he engaged these absent people in conversation as though they were beside him and he was seeing them.

This experience was a very terrifying one for the family, but it encouraged them to keep closer to Jesus. After the prayer session, the church leadership recommended that Mr. West be taken to the David Memorial Hospital. Ranlene was most hesitant since that was and still is a privately run hospital. It is administered by the Seventh-day Adventist Church. However, with much guidance she heeded and he was hospitalised. He spent approximately two weeks and was recuperating nicely. Mary Jane however, said the recuperation is not as quick as she desired, hence she requested his discharge. Her request was objected by Ranlene and this posed further contention between the two families. She misbehaved greatly at the hospital and the administration suggested that Ranlene grant her the request.

During the time of Charlie's hospitalization Mary Jane and her friends and relatives visited Ranlene's home every day at 12 noon and they displayed at the home using numerous expletives and derogatory words. Ranlene and her family went through this period with great sadness. The church members were supportive and they tried their best to constantly provide support.

In the meantime the patient's health deteriorated significantly. One day after there was a seemingly calm period; Ranlene received a verbal message indicating that her husband would like to see her and the family. Her siblings and daughter were reluctant to oblige the visit so she went with Delroy. The visit went well. Charlie was decked with jewellery that served as protection against evil spirits. He expressed to his wife that he experienced great discomfort and he was rather displeased at the way things evolved in his life, especially with the purposeful exclusion of his matrimonial family. He was elated to see his wife and he was excited to see his son. He spent most of the time of the visit talking and engaging his son's attention. All good things really come to an end, it was time for them to part and they were both sad, he cried when his wife and son left his presence that evening.

Ranlene did not cry but her heart was heavy with sadness. She cried so many times previously that it seemed she had no more tears. She was hopeful that her husband was going to recovery and be reintegrated into the family. This was nothing but a mere thought as time progressed and revealed a different reality.

Time went by and she remained quite hopeful. She consistently prayed and fervently hoped for the day her husband would return. One day while at home with the family, she heard a knock on the door, it was still very early in the morning so she enquired, "Who is there?" She heard a very familiar voice so she went to the door with some questions, "where did it happen and at what time?" the messenger tried to engage her in conversation but she was determined to get the answers to her question. He had to answer her, and he did, "it happened on the way to the hospital and it was in the weee hours of this morning". As much as Ranlene was hopeful of her husband's return, his death message did not take her by surprise.

David Adolphus West was now deceased. Mary Jane and her relatives and friends collaborated and were out for a grand show down. Little did they know that Ranlene was born into a very supportive family. They encircled her during her time of bereavement and they encamped round about her while the Lord gave His Angels charge over her and '*touch not*' was written on her. They went to the mortuary and things did not go as they planned. They were unable to access the body and they had to patiently await the arrival of his wife, who was accompanied by a group of able bodied relatives. They expressed themselves indecently but Ranlene refused to stoop to their level.

After Mr. West died the landlord of the house the family lived in had given them eviction notice. Thirty-five (35) Norton Street Lodge that everyone knew as their home was soon to be changed. Ranlene was too stressed to even consider where they would go. Her paternal grandmother having heard about her plight hastened her efforts to get the tenants out of her house. As God would have it, the tenants who were reluctant to move previously did so immediately. The house was then made available for Ranlene and her family. They moved from a one bedroom house with 'pit latrin[12]' to a three bedroom house with flush toilet and tiled bathroom. There were some repairs to be done to the house but the family was still grateful. The house was not in a deplorable condition. It was many times better than what they experienced in Lodge. Life in South was another reason to say, Thank you Jesus!

When the terrible experiences of Lodge were considered, south was a 'bed of roses[13] It was very good offer to move from where they lived, it helped Ranlene with her grieving process. She was in a new environment; new home and her experiences were being recorded on a new scroll. While the memories were still vibrant, the new experiences aided her excellent coping skills. She reminisced constantly about her husband and

---

[12] Outside toilet

[13] A term used in reference to a situation or activity that is confortable or easy)

through the strength of God she was able to experience the stages of grief and she recovered and received healing well

*"From nothing to something"*

# Test

The death of Mr. West was really stressful and the Landlord and his relatives used this opportunity to take advantage of the already weak family. They gave Ranlene a very short and inconsiderate eviction notice. She knew not where she was going but she trusted God. She told Him to take the wheel.

# Testimony

Ranlene and her siblings and children received a bigger and better house that accommodated them well, fostering growth and development in every family member. When God blesses you no one can curse you. He takes you with nothing from nowhere and gives you something and takes you everywhere.

**Revelation 3:8** *"I know your works. See, I have set before you an open door, and no one can shut it; for you have a little strength, have kept My word, and have not denied My name.*

She received the call from her grandmother the day before her husband was buried telling her that the house is available and she can go and occupy same. "I do not want any rent from you just ensure you keep the house clean" in less than a week after the burial, the family was out of the one bedroom house to a three bedroom house. The compound was filled with fruit trees and the neighbourhood was totally different, peace and tranquillity. This was nothing short of God's blessing.

The family enjoyed the new community, and the space in their new home. Everyone became involved in the house and yard cleaning exercises. The fruit trees were pruned and the yields were fantastic. Cherries and mangoes were always on the trees. La-Toya took pleasure in climbing the trees and the fruits picked were shared with neighbours and relatives.

Life started feeling lonely for her. The daily activities were very mundane, work, work and more work. Ranlene's support system was weak. It consisted of a few persons who were unable to help themselves, more so, to even help her. After relationships failed because of lack of trust, dishonestly and several other reasons she decided to remain single. Many individuals were attracted to the home since it was predominantly populated by young beautiful females. Her parental instincts allowed her to prevent cases of sexual abuse with males who wanted to prey on her sisters. This has propelled her to remain single for a very long time. A brother in Christ recommended a male friend for her. She decided to accept the recommendation since this was promised to alleviate her stresses through companionship. Wanting to be stress free, she willingly agreed to get to know the individual better.

"Run from the hot oil into the fire" this was the best way to explain her decision. As Guyanese would say; 'Ranlene run from the coffin and butt up wid de jumbie'[14]. The friendship went well until she consented to a relationship. Dishonesty was often present in their interaction. Her male companion told lies for no apparent reason. He was poorly trained and she was often embarrassed whenever they were at formal settings. His

---

[14] An expression that means someone gets outs of a difficult or bad situation and eventually gets into a more difficult or worse one.

etiquette was on par with a four year old or in some cases was really similar to a toddler. This encouraged her to have several training conversations with him. She even allowed him opportunities within the home to learn. He agreed to improve and would often apologised, however when given the opportunity he displayed other poor training behaviours. This among many other issues and conflicts has forced her to end the relationship. She already had several things dealing with. She had her children and siblings to train and care for, this instead of alleviating her stress increased it.

Her children never approved her relationship with the gentleman. Having received the teachings from their mother, they thought her choice was not in alignment with the teachings. They highlighted several reasons for the relationship to end. Some of the reasons were underlined with their mother, highlighted their jealousy. They loved and still love their mother dearly and did not want to share her love with anyone outside of their immediate family circle. Her children played many tricks on the gentleman but he was rather patient and persistent, he went through all the challenges in the children's eyes:

he passed none! He tried asserting his fatherly authority but this was mocked and greeted with; you are not our father! They vehemently made that fact known at each visit he made to the house. He eventually learnt that he either worked with the children or work against them and choosing the last was to his detriment.

The struggle was real for Ranlene, challenges with her interaction and the male companion as well as challenges with the rest of the family and him. She was not ready for these heights of difficulties. Even though she wanted companionship she was willing to remain single and stress free in that regard. She went back to her routine of life without any social attachments. During these years she worked as labour woman within construction, cleaner, washer, domestic helper among other domestic related work. She did all of these just to ensure that her children and siblings were provided for.

At this time some of her siblings have grown to become young adults, Laundiss and Malinie were with her throughout all the struggles. Garfield was in and out of the interior of Guyana working as a Pork knocker. He sparsely contributed financially to the household.

Ohdarry and Stacey were with their father and the family continued to exist on the mercy of God.

Many males also sought to take advantage of the family because the only male was Delroy who was but a toddler. Ranlene in all instances stood up to the males to represent her family. There was a particular male neighbour who was very troublesome. He used expletives at the front of the family's home and said several threatening statements. One evening while Ranlene was at work, her siblings noticed something strange; it was only the said morning the man threatened Ranlene. The young ladies realised the man was armed and was proceeding towards the shortcut where Ranlene was expected to walk on her way home. They became scared and they devised a plan quickly. Cell phones were not the accessory of the day, even if it was; this family definitely could not afford any. One of her sisters snuck behind him and realised he was waiting at a dark spot. This forced them to wait for her at the head of the shortcut and they all walked around the longer route. After waiting for a very long time, the man passed the house and remarked, "yuh lucky ah never ketch yuh".

This was enough reasons for action to be taken against this individual. Ranlene is a very smart woman; she did not challenge him in any physical way. She stayed quietly inside, and sought advice. She followed what was said to her and a report was made to the police station. The individual was punished by law and the family remained at peace.

Ranlene led her family in a respectable way. Young men had to write and ask home for her sisters and daughter. She set the standard for their courtship experience really high. This influenced her being able to experience their marriage and sharing the joy of them having children after marriage. It was a joy to witness her sisters' marriages. The family size decreased and Ranlene was prepared to begin counting her blessings. How far will she go with the counting? She had many dreams, imagination and aspirations, what direction will her life take, only God knew.

# Chapter Five

## "After a Storm comes calm"

Success comes after hard work. This is a proven fact. However, during her trials this fact seemed improbable to Ranlene. They were working hard towards their goal when her husband became sick. Now it seems like they were unable to build their desired home. After all, this project has been stalled for several years. During the time when work commenced on the property Delroy was a foetus, he has now matured into a handsome twenty-five year old and the house is still incomplete. Ranlene made several unsuccessful attempts to get assistance for the building of their home. Most lending entities informed her that, her salary she earned was insufficient to afford her a loan. As faith turned for the worst, one day Ranlene's brother, Garfield went to weed the land and was greeted by a notice: **"NO TRESPASSING, Owner of this property MUST report to the Ministry of Housing Immediately."**

Overcome with a strange feeling of apprehension and optimism, Ranlene's thoughts began to race. Could this be the gateway of her breakthrough? Did the Ministry of Housing find out she was unable to build and were offering her some form of subsidy? Many thoughts clouded her mind, but she was definitely not prepared for the startling news she was about to receive.

She was greeted and treated quite politely at the Ministry of Housing. After identifying herself and purpose for her visit The staff at the Ministry was shocked at the number of property documents she had in her possession.

One employee further explained that the notice was in the newspapers for weeks asking the owner to step forward. Ranlene was surprised since she was totally unaware of this new revelation. The staff further revealed their evaluation office had no record of the place being valued. Her land was sold, according to the staff. What was most interesting about the last bit of information shared was, the price the land was sold for mirrored the valuation cost rather closely.

Ranlene did not know what to believe since she was bombarded by deception. This experience reinforced the truth that we truly live in a wicked world. Helpless, dejected, hopeless, depressed, disadvantaged were a few adjectives that described Ranlene's feeling at the moment. She was further, advised to return to the Ministry within two weeks.

In a desperate effort to get guidance, she aimlessly walked into a lawyer's office after leaving the Ministry and she relayed her ordeal. The lawyer seeking a golden opportunity immediately presented how he was going to handle the case and requested a down payment from Ranlene to precede. "Down payment" echoed and all she could think of was' "I don't have any money". Her thoughts were verbalised and the lawyer boldly and insensitively replied, "no money no business Ma'am" She was now walking the streets without any direction. As she walked aimlessly down the street she passed the office of a well-known Lawyer, the Late Benjamin Gibson. She saw him on the road and he casually asked, "How are you?" Frustration took precedence in her response and he invited her inside the office to talk a bit more.   He was shocked to hear what had happened. Ironically, he provided legal representation to David West years before so he knew Ranlene.  At the brink of her frustration, Mr Gibson willingly offered to provide legal services without any down payment, subsequently, arrangements were made and the process commenced..

Two weeks had passed and Ranlene returned to the Ministry, she was appalled at the hostility that greeted her this time.. Then the reality hit her, the property she worked so hard for with her late husband David to maintain was now at the centre of a heated disputed.  There were two owners of the one property. The Ministry of Housing had resold her land. She was asked to return within two weeks to negotiate for another plot of land, where they were relocating her to the West Bank Demerara, Guyana. She strongly objected to this proposal. Not only was the suggested plot of land in a remote area, where there were no access road, electricity or water, but the plot under dispute had sentimental values attached.

When she returned as was requested she was literally chased out of the office of a prominent worker who happens to be there even at this moment. "Get out of my office!" The worker continued, I asked you to return and your lawyer sent us a letter? Go back to him and have him represent you." By this time Ranlene was not the emotional wreck she was two weeks prior. She left and immediately dialogued with her lawyer who encouraged her, "don't worry this is your land and we will nicely ask them to return it".

The Ministry of Housing sold Ranlene's land to another individual, a sibling of one of her neighbours. After neighbours saw years passing and nothing was being done, one person encouraged their sibling to buy the land. The land was illegally acquired through the Ministry of Housing. She had all the relevant documents to prove that she was the rightful owner. The only document was outstanding was her Transport. Believe it or not every time she went to enquire about her transport she was told it was not yet ready. At that time the then Government took a very long time to provide owners with their land titles, so Ranlene was waiting for years on the title. Surprisingly though, the second owner's transport was being processed. Irregularities and corruption were the orders of the day. As corrupt as things were God has been an on time God to Ranlene and her family.

She engaged the support of her church family and they prayed constantly. Ranlene could not believe this was the reality. It seemed rather unfortunate that the trials were coming with considerable frequency. After acquiring her legal fees and with much consistent prayer, the judge mandated The Ministry of Housing to commence and complete process of issuing the Transport for Ranlene West. With much prayer, hard work, perseverance, determination, commitment and dedication victory was Ranlene's.

The Late Lawyer Gibson did an excellent job in representing his client, Ranlene; she received full ownership to her **294 Plot PP Lamaha Park, East La Penitence Lot**. This was really great that the land for which she toiled hard with her deceased husband was regained. She had enough reasons to give praises to God. After the legal matter was resolved she was able to pay for the land to be fenced. It was her desire to begin building but with her children still at school, she was unable to do so. She effortlessly tried to get her house built and every avenue she tried proved closed. There was not a legal, moral or acceptable way that she did not try to get money for her house to build her house. She had exhausted all her efforts. Having received a several disappointments she resorted to giving up. She concluded that God will do it at His time. She prayed earnestly: daily, weekly, monthly and yearly hoping that something can be done for her land. Despite her efforts, all she was able to do was weed, clear, burn and offer a stipend for someone to clean when necessary.

# Chapter Six

## "Never Forgotten, God knows my name"

Her siblings have all married, daughter migrated to study and she remained at home with Delroy. Everyone has grown and started their families and she still remained unable to build her desired home. Delroy was still in school. He was in his teen now displaying the rebellious phase of adolescence, his behaviour sometimes frustrated Ranlene but she never gave up on him. She remained supportive, loving and constantly prayerful. While the difficult period seemed to have been gradually subsiding, challenges were still evident but not as intense.

Receiving letters via post was a pleasant thing for this family. This was how they communicated mainly with their relatives and friends overseas. While there were times when the only mails received were bills, it was always a joy to receive a letter from someone overseas. Having collected a letter by post, she realised it was from her grandmother, she started opening a little faster. This time the letter was not one of the usually pleasantries: how is everyone doing? Was not the kind of questions asked in the letter, it was a rather informative one. 'Granny' as she was fondly called informed her that she has decided to WILL the house Ranlene was living in to her two elder granddaughters. She further explained that the eldest will get the upper flat and the elder will get the lower flat that will be enclosed and renovated.

This was great news for Ranlene understanding that she was still unable to build on her piece of land. She welcomed this news. Unfortunately, another letter came some months later, indicating that plans have changed. Apparently, Lydia decided to WILL the house to her grandchildren without getting her children's approval, so the decision was revoked. The decision was now taken to sell the property. Having lived and cared for the house for sixteen years, Ranlene felt privileged that she would have been given preference to purchase the house. In faith, with the assistance of her children and siblings, she aggressively pursued  immediate cash, for the purchase. However, to her dismay, the next news she heard about the house was that it was sold. Are you for real, is this truly happening? Why does this have to be me? Oh God, this is too much? Matters got worse when she knew who the buyer was, the phone rang one day and she answered "oh hi Ranlin, this is your uncle Desmond," Ranlene's voice immediately dipped and her heart started beating faster. The telephone call was one to inform her that Uncle Desmond is the new owner and in a twist of fortune she was required to move.

A few weeks went by and Ranlene's pressure started rising. Everyone knew she was in search of a house to live. Almost everyone had the same response, "the time given to you to find a place is way too short." The fact still remained that she had to move. Since she was not getting through with any affordable house, she started asking persons to keep her furniture. Once again, life took a drastic spiral downhill. It was extremely rough on her.  Delroy started living in the south Ruimveldt[15]

---

[15] The name of a place in Georgetown

when he was eight months old and he was now in high school. This situation impacted him greatly. He was hurt to see his mother hurt and there wasn't anything he could have done. Ranlene and Delroy were home one day when a car stopped at the house. They were both not expecting anyone, so they did not pay much attention. Ranlene was astonished! It was Desmond Grannum and his wife.......who gained entry to the yard through the unlock gate, came upstairs and greeted Ranlene and Delroy briefly. Without hesitation, he made it known that he needs his house since he would like to begin reconstruction. The interaction shared with Ranlene was hostile and by this time Ranlene's stress level escalated further. So she snapped at him, "Gosh! Can someone be so wicked? It's not that I don't want to move it's hard for me to get a place, as you can notice my furniture are all packed and ready to move." Desmond was definitely not expecting this response. His wife immediately exited the building while he shakily prepared to follow her. Ranlene intensified her search as she was desperate for the Grannums to get their house. Everyone far and wide knew the urgency of the house request. Offers began to come that were out of Georgetown. Understanding that Delroy was preparing for Secondary School Exams, she was cautioned against long distances. It seemed as all hope was lost and just when she was about to give up, something divinely-led happened. A family from church was in transition mode from one house to the next and instead of renting the house with the usual conditions and principles; they adjusted these for Ranlene and her son. Isn't God awesome? Ranlene's siblings facilitated an emergency meeting and the decisions were sealed. They moved from 3352 Canal Place South Ruimveldt Park where everyone called home to Campbellville. Changes are just inevitable.

The neighbourhood was different. The house was situated in a more business oriented community. The peace of night rests was invaded by loud music that emanated from a night spot, two buildings away. Having thought about the torture experienced previously, the noise certainly was not bothersome. With little or no delay Ranlene met the neighbours.

Although now at ease, Ranlene still dreamt of her own home, she often optimistically expressed preferences about how she would like her house to be. As impossible as this seemed to others, she was adamant that God will one day open the doors of heaven and pour out her blessings in copious measures for her house to be built.

## "Provision of needs"

## Test

Three months is not a very long time to find a new place to live, moreover, one that is affordable. They had not paid rent for over sixteen years, yet this was now the new reality. It seemed impossible.

## Testimony

God provided the church family to bless her with a three bedroom house in Central Georgetown. The house was very close to church and the space was much better than the house in South. There were more fruit trees. This experience helped Ranlene to understand that God take you from great to greater. God is AWESOME!

**Philippians 4:***19 And my God shall supply all your needs, according to His riches in Christ Jesus.*

Ranlene lived in Campbellville for four years. Life was better there than it was in the latter years in South. Things were a bit better, Ranlene lived with her son and four relatives until the relatives moved and the two remained alone. During these times Delroy prepared for Secondary School Examination and passed with grades one and two in seven subjects! The young man everyone except Ranlene gave up on, shone brilliantly. Challenges came and challenges went but Ranlene and her son remained committed to God.

**Old fire stick easy fuh ketch[16]**

A gentleman Ranlene once dated resurfaced. At this time he appeared more mature and Ranlene was still single and of course ready to mingle. After all her house was empty, Delroy being a sociable person was more out than in the home. She was now in a better position to tolerate him and he seemed changed. She decided to take her chances.

---

[16] Old relationships between former lovers can easily be rekindled.

## "He never gives up on us"

# Test

Delroy was going through one of the many challenging times adolescents experience. His challenge was a mixture of psychological distress, perpetuated by what was happening with his mother and relatives coupled with his developmental phase. The teachings he received were outweighed by his social influences.

# Testimony

When everyone gave up on Delroy, his prayerful mother did not. His sister was determined to see him shine. His aunts saw a gentleman while others saw a thug. Nothing happens before God's time. In His time everything will work out for the best.

*1 Samuel 16:7 "Do not look at his appearance or at his physical stature, because I have refused him. For the Lord does not see as man sees; man looks at the outward appearance, but the Lord looks at the heart."*

Having successfully passed seven CXCs with grades 1 and 2, Delroy was on a job search for nine (9) months and no progress was forthcoming. He became despondent and frustrated and was getting rather desperate. Just when he was about to give up a door was opened. He always wanted to be a pilot. This was his time to shine. He attended the interview and got through immediately after the interview. This felt like heaven for him. After working for only one week he was asked to work on the seventh day of the week. *Was this some trick or something? How can this be? Gosh……..* Delroy shared the challenge with his mother hoping she would help him come to a decision she boldly responded, "I have done my part with teaching you, now you have to showcase what you learnt with your decision." He made the long and hard decision to keep his job and was determined to tell his boss the great news. As he went to give the news he was convicted to do otherwise. His boss asked him, "You are giving up such a great paying job for a church?" Delroy's decision was final and he walked peacefully out of the organisation. Delroy had no clue that his mother was praying from the time he approached her for her input in the decision until he returned home. She is a prayer warrior. Delroy gave up that job and was back in the unemployment bracket, looking for a job. He was examining his options when he received an invitation for an interview. He was employed following the interview. However, it was on a contractual basis, the job paid well; just before that contract expired, he received the good news that the contract will be renewed. This renewal was certainly not what God had planned for him since he received another letter for an interview at a leading commercial bank. The bank had a better offer which he accepted. Within one year Delroy had received three promotions. Currently, he's serving as a Personal Loan Officer; this intelligent young man has won the heart of many through his infectious smile. He is engaged to be married and has a very brilliant future ahead of him. He has made and continues to make his mother super proud. Ranlene's hard work has paid off.

## *"We serve an on time God"*

# Test

No job! After job searching for nine months the result was nothing. When a job was finally given, his Sabbath conviction was tested. Several offers came, some of which were not morally right, what did he do?

# Testimony

He stood firmly for what he believed and He purposed in his heart to represent God in all that he did. He rejected the offer from an aeronautic entity, having vested much interest in being a Pilot. He believes that God will lead and take him to where he wants him to be. He is in a job that does not interfere with his Sabbath keeping conviction.

***Deuteronomy 11:25*** *– "No one will be able to stand against you, The Lord your God He has promised you, will put the terror and fear of you on the whole land wherever you go."*

# Chapter Seven

**"Newness of life"**

Ranlene has now found love on a two way street. She was ready and inspired to make strides with Craig. They decided to begin a relationship. Things moved slowly and comfortably so they made plans to take it to a different level. They agreed to be married. Ranlene noticed some slight changes but she totally overlooked the signs. Craig being unemployed for several years opted to go to Barbados, where he would be able to work and save towards the wedding.

The prospective couple had some challenges but Ranlene was very understanding. She believed that compromise was necessary so she overlooked many things. She was very grateful for the commonality in the shared denominational faith. While he did not have long term plans and goals Ranlene was still patient and understanding.

Preparations began from Ranlene's end for the wedding. Invitations were distributed and everyone far and near were highly expectant of the occasion. La-Toya travelled from Jamaica for the wedding, the home was buzzing with the excitement. Prior to the wedding week, Craig was expected to travel two weeks before but the flight was constantly postponed according to him. He called after every postponement to explain why he was unable to travel.

The nerves began to rock as the week of the wedding was here and the groom was still not in the country. Three days, two days, one day, before the wedding, then the phone rang quite normally. The caller having being identified as Craig requested speaking with his wife to be. He was denied this access since all he has done was to provide reasons that were empty and Ranlene's blood pressure was elevating. La-Toya related to him and it was understood that he was unable to travel for the following day. His explanation was poor immigration communication and completion of document signing.

The damage was done and damage control had to be enforced. All the guests were called and informed that the wedding has been postponed until further notice. Ranlene's speech was now withheld and her interactions were little or in some case none. She was unresponsive to questions asked and comments shared. She was staring in space repeatedly.

The family worked collaboratively in the best interest of Ranlene. As such, the family challenges were contained and the guests were informed only what they needed to know. Several persons were quite inquisitive and were hesitant to accept the reason given for the postponement.

Ranlene in chagrin and exasperation was still forgiving. She accepted several other dates set by Craig, all of which he never abided by. This was the time that the decision had to be made. She had given him an ultimatum and he was now ready to proceed with the relationship. Ranlene told him he should set a date that he will work with or move on with his life. He readily agreed and was willing to make things work. He made all the agreements while he was still in Barbados. However, having heard what was Ranlene's decision he was booked to travel within short time. Everyone watched to see if he would really arrive. She had already made her mind to perhaps remain single if not forever, for the time being. Bright and early in December 2011 **Craig Winston Gibbons** made his arrival at the Cheddi Jagan International Airport. Arrangements were reactivated and the wedding was convened within one week. On the twenty second day of December, 2011 Ranlene and Craig said "I do" to each other. After all the hurdles they were now ready to show the world how much they love each other. They were determined to be bonded forever. After twenty two years she has rekindled a fire to last forever. It was a memorable day, she was ready to experience the happily ever after that many stories include.

*Ranlene beautifully dressed on her wedding day.*

### Shattered Dreams Chaotic Reality

Having enjoyed a few months of marital bliss, the reality was now staring at Ranlene: Craig was not consistently employed. One would ask why Ranlene proceeded with the marriage to this man that showed numerous red flags. However, she was convinced; he was now a change man. However, it seemed the only change he made was in the tone of his voice. When he returned to Guyana, he had taken full responsibility of the rent for the Campbellville house. He stepped up to the plate a few times but the old irresponsible him returned.

### The Struggle is real

One month went by and the rent was not paid, it happened the second time. At this time Ranlene began to get flustered. She told him that he needed to get a job and be able to provide for his family. He reluctantly agreed to do all she requested. Delroy being the only consistent worker of the family managed to take care of the essentials, provision of food, payment of bills and any other expense that they had. As time progressed and nothing was forthcoming, Craig suggested returning to

Barbados where he would be able to send money for his wife. She agreed mainly because of desperation. He was packed and was off.

Phone calls came and the communication was good. There was great news he stepped up to his words and money was sent. This was awesome! Things seem a bit better. The over rent were paid and they were moving steadily with the other expenses. Ranlene was a bit relaxed. During this time she began her search for employment to assist Delroy with the expenses but Delroy did not agree, hence she stayed at home. She assisted with some babysitting duties for which she was adequately remunerated. This income was helpful in many ways. However, both babysitting jobs were short lived as the children were enrolled into the school system. Things were really progressing nicely. Ranlene became very hopeful and though he must be working really hard to pay two debts and fulfil his matrimonial responsibility simultaneously.

Ranlene is a blessed woman and has received many directions from God through dreams. She, however, turned a blind eye to some of the dreams she received prior to their wedding. Was she naïve, stubborn or just determined to get marry? The dreams that penetrated her mind were one: she was at the top floor of a three storeyed building and after she became married her husband held her hands and brought her to the ground floor. The floor she was on was fully furnished and he brought her to the ground floor that was total empty. While she was trying to understand that dream, the following night she dreamt her legs were paining and when she went to the doctor, as her legs were being held for examination, the doctor's hand went into her foot that was very hallow. After the Doctors hands sunk in the foot, it was revealed that her shin bone was filled with the parasite wood ants. Thank the heavens this was just a dream. It seemed like Ranlene needed Biblical Joseph to give her some interpretations. Strange enough, all her dreams were provided with explanations. As creepy as it was in the dream, the reality was seriously the same. While her bones hadn't wood ants[17] the trails she experienced were just as devastating.

---

[17] Scientific name: Formica rufa also called horse ant

Craig called to say the money was sent and this added some relief to Ranlene. The person arrived in Guyana with only 150US. Ranlene questioned if that was all the money they received and it certainly was. Efforts to reach Craig proved futile. Ranlene used the money she received and paid the smaller debt leaving the greater debt and the rent. She was then informed that the person who brought the money was owed as well, and their money was deducted. The greater debtor cancelled the debt, all praises to God. This left the rent as the only expense to be aid. That marked another unpaid month. The family's inability to pay the rent heightened and they were given notice to vacate the premises.

Ranlene's blood pressure skyrocketed. While Delroy tried to hold the fort, he was still young and as such the burden was humongous. They eventually found a place that was outside of Georgetown and they were living comfortably. While the place was not their ideal, they were managing the rent and were living quite humbly.

Craig called some months after and as usual he had all the apologies and every reason why his wife should forgive him. She was very upset and was indecisive of going ahead with the marriage. Relatives and friends offered her many different suggestions. She fasted and prayed and asked God to show her again what He wanted her to do. Time flew bye and Craig continued living in Barbados, he made many more promises, none forthcoming but he thrived on lies and dishonesty. His beautiful wife had made her decision that she was preparing for a divorce.

### *While man disappoints God appoints*

La-Toya called her mother in January 2013 to share the exciting news of the addition to their family. She then requested the presence of her mother in Jamaica with her family to participate in the birth of her first grandchild. This was exciting news for Ranlene. She consented without any hesitation. Soon she was off to Jamaica in November of 2013. She experienced the birth of Jenae and was extremely supportive to the Tuckers as they welcomed a bouncing baby girl into their family.

Craig made contact with Ranlene while she was in Jamaica and requested that she prepared to return to Guyana where they can resolve their differences and resume living together. All the promises were empty as usual. Ranlene refused to inform him about her return date to Guyana. In an effort to demonstrate that he means what he says, he took the first step and went back to Guyana. He was supposed to travel with the total of five months' rent for the house in Campbellville. He returned to Guyana with several pieces of old clothing and an enormous amount of disposal plastic that he has retained.

Having spent nine months in Jamaica, Ranlene had departed for Guyana unknowing to her husband. To her surprise, when she arrived, her home on the East Coast was transformed to a garbage disposal site. The place smelled horrible, there were damaged things, dirty things all mixed together. It was at this time that Ranlene realised something was inherently wrong with her husband. Not only was he mentally sick but he was physically sick as well.

She was too empathetic and loving to provide him with a divorce. She decided to work with him despite his challenges. She sought counselling for them, engaged him in much discussion and he recovered nicely or at least so it seemed. She tirelessly encouraged him to get a job. Persons tried getting jobs for him and he found every possible reason to reject them. He spent many days at a prominent market in Georgetown, where he collected food in the afternoons and returned home. The food he brought was either spoilt, remnants of a meal or just dirty.

Ranlene sought employment at a restaurant while Craig remained at home. She worked very hard. At evening her feet were swollen and her blood pressure was constantly high. As a result, she visited the doctor frequently. Her children then decided that she should desist from working. She insisted on doing otherwise, until she was unfairly treated by her boss and her employment was forcefully ended. With much guidance and suggestion, providing her resignation was the better thing to do and she certainly did.

Craig moved from staying at home to idling during the day. He never saw what others tried to show him. His health deteriorated rapidly. He spent more than three months visiting the doctors doing numerous tests. One day while everyone was home he was returned from the streets in a taxi. He overdosed himself with multivitamins and pain medication and collapsed at a worksite that she frequently visited. He was cared for and was seemingly better. Ranlene having received her visa was treated to two months in the USA.

While she was in the USA Ranlene received some devastating news about Craig. His sickness was now in a deplorable state upon her return, she spent many days visiting him. He no longer lived in the same house with her, since he moved out while she was away. His health was very poor and moving him back to the house was not the best choice. Understanding that her grandchildren were there and the distance they lived from the city, it was better for him to be in Central Georgetown to readily be able to access health services.

She faithfully visited him weekly and cared for him. He was never a person to make bold independent decision and even throughout his sickness that was constantly seen. He cried profusely through his sickness, several startling confessions were shared, matters affecting his family and him as an individual and a spiritual being. On December 9, 2017, he gave his last breath. He gave up the fight of life to death.

Ranlene prayed endlessly asking God how long more will she remain in the marriage. Her marriage life had now ended and all she could say, "God is truly faithful" while many person may not have understood her response. It is only who feels it knows it. Craig left several debts and no money to pay them. Ranlene was not worried she was more confident to know that God will make a way where there seemed to be no way.

*"It's not over until God says it is over"*

## Test

Craig took sick and after some months of illness, he died. He died leaving no **WILL** but a Humongous **BILL**.

## Testimony

His relatives rose to the occasion and took charge of **ALL** funeral expenses. The only thing Ranlene was expected to do was dress and attend the funeral. Death announcement, burial spot, casket everything were all covered. It was paid in full a reminder of how our sins were paid in full by King Jesus. When we stand for God He stands for us.

*1 Corinthians 10:13 – No temptation has overtaken you except such as is common to man; but God is faithful, who will not allow you to be tempted beyond what you are able but with the temptation will also make the way of escape that you may be able to bear it. Great and Joyous news!*

In the following year, January 2018, God started with awesomeness, the loan to build their home was approved. With great; commitment, dedication, perseverance and support the house construction commenced in March, with an expected finish in July. God is always God. He answers our prayers in His time. As Ranlene reflected upon God's goodness she became worried having been diagnosed with mild pneumonia in April. She was taken to the hospital and several tests were done on her after she had an asthma attack. To God be the glory! All tests were done and results revealed that she is well and healthy. With her asthma being controlled and blood pressure being monitored, she is good as new. She is now single and free. In her words, "I would love to have a companion but I am in no hurry." God will make a way for her. **She moved into her own home on June 2018. This was a blessing!**

God has great plans for her and for everyone if only they trust Him and allows Him to lead their live. God is able to do exceeding more and abundant than we can think ask or imagine.

*Photographic Highlights*

Ranlene and her two sisters, they share one mother one father

Ranlene her daughter and two grandchildren: Jenae & Jediel

*Ranlene, her father and two sisters*

Ranlene and her two sisters, they
share one mother one father

Ranlene and her siblings from left: Malinie, Laundiss, Garvy and Stacey sitting

*Ranlene at 50*

Nothing is better than a mother son moment

# *Blessings over Flow*

**(Ranlene's Family house erected and on the verge of completion)**

# References

Stockan, J. A., & Robinson, E. J.H.  (2016). *Wood ant ecology and conservation.*  New York: Cambridge University Press.

The Holy Bible New King James Version

(Definition of "Chain smokers" from the Cambridge Advanced Learner's Dictionary and Thesaurus @ Cambridge University Press (2018)

Definition of obeah man from Merriam Webster Dictionary. Retrieved from www.merriam-webster.com on June 24, 2018

A bed of roses, (n.d) Farlex Dictionary of Idioms (2015). Retrieved on June 24, 2018 from http://idioms.thefreedictionary.com

Printed in the United States
By Bookmasters